Information

MY FAMILY NEEDS TO KNOW

I0869394

new seasons®
a division of Publications International, Ltd

Louis Weber, CEO
Publications International, Ltd.
8140 Lehigh Ave
Morton Grove, IL 60053

Images from Shutterstock.com

ISBN: 978-1-63938-864-6

Manufactured in China.

8 7 6 5 4 3 2 1

CONTENTS

WHAT MY FAMILY NEEDS TO KNOW

This practical organizer is designed to make all your important information available in one place. It is vital that loved ones know the precise location of this information in the event of your incapacity or death. Then they can be sure that your wishes are known and followed and your assets are protected. By taking some time now to answer the questions and fill in the blanks, you will likely save your loved ones hours, days, weeks, or even months later on.

It's also important to keep this information up-to-date. We recommend revisiting this at least once a year. For things that are likely to change, you might want to write in pencil to make it easier to update.

Since everything of importance will be listed in the following pages, this organizer becomes the first thing your loved ones must have. It is the road map to everything else. Therefore, you should tell trusted loved ones where to find this organizer. Let them know that if something happens to you, this is where they should start.

Today's date: ____________

MY PERSONAL INFORMATION

This includes all pertinent personal and family information as of the above date.

My full legal name: ______________________________

Any aliases: ______________________________

Date of birth: ________________ Place of birth: ______________________

Social Security number: _________ - ________ - ___________

Marital status: ☐ Single ☐ Married ☐ Separated: Date ________________

☐ Divorced: Date _______________ ☐ Widowed: Date ______________

Street address: ______________________________

City: ______________________ State: ______ Zip Code: ______________

County: ______________________________

Phone(s): ______________________ ______________________ ______________________

Home Cell Work

E-mail: ______________________________

I am a citizen of: ______________________________

My Spouse (if married)

Spouse's full legal name: ____________________

Date of birth: ____________ Place of birth: ____________

Social Security number: ______ - ______ - ______

Phone: ____________ E-mail: ____________

Citizen of: ____________________

My Children (if any)

Name: ____________ Date of birth: ____________

Address: ____________________

Phone: ____________ E-mail: ____________

Name: ____________ Date of birth: ____________

Address: ____________________

Phone: ____________ E-mail: ____________

Name: ____________ Date of birth: ____________

Address: ____________________

Phone: ____________ E-mail: ____________

Name: ____________ Date of birth: ____________

Address: ____________________

Phone: ____________ E-mail: ____________

Name: ____________ Date of birth: ____________

Address: ____________________

Phone: ____________ E-mail: ____________

Name: ____________ Date of birth: ____________

Address: ____________________

Phone: ____________ E-mail: ____________

MY EMERGENCY CONTACTS

Name: ________________ Relationship: ________________
Address: ________________________________
Phone: ________________ E-mail: ________________

Name: ________________ Relationship: ________________
Address: ________________________________
Phone: ________________ E-mail: ________________

Name: ________________ Relationship: ________________
Address: ________________________________
Phone: ________________ E-mail: ________________

MY ADVANCE DIRECTIVES

An advance directive is a legal document, such as a living will or health care power of attorney, that expresses your wishes regarding medical treatment in the event you become incapacitated. A living will (or instruction directive) alerts health care providers what type of medical treatment you want to receive or refuse. You should also appoint a trusted person (called a health care agent or proxy) to make medical decisions for you when you cannot.

My Health Care Agent(s)

I have named the following person(s) to make health care decisions for me if I cannot.

1. Name: ________________ Relationship: ________________
Address: ________________________________
Phone: ________________ E-mail: ________________

2. Name: ________________ Relationship: ________________
Address: ________________________________
Phone: ________________ E-mail: ________________

My Agent(s) for Property and Financial Matters

I have named the following person(s) to handle my property and other financial matters if I am unable to do so.

1. Name: ________________ Relationship: ________________
Address: ________________________________
Phone: ________________ E-mail: ________________

2. Name: ________________ Relationship: ________________
Address: ________________________________
Phone: ________________ E-mail: ________________

Location of advance directive documents: ________________

MY MEDICAL HISTORY

Current Medical Issues

Illness or medical issue: ______________________________

Symptoms: ______________________________

Doctor: ______________________________

Treatments, hospitalizations, and/or surgeries: ______________________________

____

Notes: ______________________________

Illness or medical issue: ______________________________

Symptoms: ______________________________

Doctor: ______________________________

Treatments, hospitalizations, and/or surgeries: ______________________________

____

Notes: ______________________________

Illness or medical issue: ______________________________

Symptoms: ______________________________

Doctor: ______________________________

Treatments, hospitalizations, and/or surgeries: ______________________________

____

Notes: ______________________________

Allergies: ______________________________

____

Dietary restrictions: ______________________________

____

Past Medical Issues

Illness or medical issue: ______________________________

Treatments, hospitalizations, and/or surgeries: ______________________________

____

Outcome: ______________________________

Illness or medical issue: ______________________________

Treatments, hospitalizations, and/or surgeries: ______________________________

____

Outcome: ______________________________

MY HEALTH INSURANCE

Insurance company name: ______________________________

Plan name: ______________________________

Plan type: ☐ Original Medicare ☐ Medicare Advantage ☐ Prescription Drug

☐ Medicare Supplement (Medigap) ☐ Other: ______________

Member ID #: ______________ Customer service: ______________

Insurance company name: ______________________________

Plan name: ______________________________

Plan type: ☐ Original Medicare ☐ Medicare Advantage ☐ Prescription Drug

☐ Medicare Supplement (Medigap) ☐ Other: ______________

Member ID #: ______________ Customer service: ______________

Insurance company name: ______________________________

Plan name: ______________________________

Plan type: ☐ Original Medicare ☐ Medicare Advantage ☐ Prescription Drug

☐ Medicare Supplement (Medigap) ☐ Other: ______________

Member ID #: ______________ Customer service: ______________

Insurance company name: ______________________________

Plan name: ______________________________

Plan type: ☐ Original Medicare ☐ Medicare Advantage ☐ Prescription Drug

☐ Medicare Supplement (Medigap) ☐ Other: ______________

Member ID #: ______________ Customer service: ______________

MY HEALTH CARE PROVIDERS

Primary care physician name: ______________________________

Address: ______________________________

Phone: ______________ E-mail: ______________________________

Dentist name: ______________________________

Address: ______________________________

Phone: ______________ E-mail: ______________________________

Eye care doctor name: ____________________

Address: ____________________

Phone: __________ E-mail: ____________________

Doctor name: __________ Specialty: __________

Address: ____________________

Phone: __________ E-mail: ____________________

Doctor name: __________ Specialty: __________

Address: ____________________

Phone: __________ E-mail: ____________________

Doctor name: __________ Specialty: __________

Address: ____________________

Phone: __________ E-mail: ____________________

Doctor name: __________ Specialty: __________

Address: ____________________

Phone: __________ E-mail: ____________________

Pharmacy name: ____________________

Address: ____________________

Phone: __________ Hours: __________

Website: ____________________

Login username: __________ Password: __________

Pharmacy name: ____________________

Address: ____________________

Phone: __________ Hours: __________

Website: ____________________

Login username: __________ Password: __________

Hospital name: __________ Phone: __________

Address: ____________________

Hospital name: __________ Phone: __________

Address: ____________________

MY MEDICATIONS

Prescription Medications

Name: ______________________ Dosage: ______________
Number of times per day: _____ ☐ AM ☐ PM ☐ Other: ______________
Prescribing doctor: ______________________________
Pharmacy: ______________ Prescription #: ______________
Date started: __________ Date discontinued (if any): ______________

Name: ______________________ Dosage: ______________
Number of times per day: _____ ☐ AM ☐ PM ☐ Other: ______________
Prescribing doctor: ______________________________
Pharmacy: ______________ Prescription #: ______________
Date started: __________ Date discontinued (if any): ______________

Name: ______________________ Dosage: ______________
Number of times per day: _____ ☐ AM ☐ PM ☐ Other: ______________
Prescribing doctor: ______________________________
Pharmacy: ______________ Prescription #: ______________
Date started: __________ Date discontinued (if any): ______________

Name: ______________________ Dosage: ______________
Number of times per day: _____ ☐ AM ☐ PM ☐ Other: ______________
Prescribing doctor: ______________________________
Pharmacy: ______________ Prescription #: ______________
Date started: __________ Date discontinued (if any): ______________

Name: ______________________ Dosage: ______________
Number of times per day: _____ ☐ AM ☐ PM ☐ Other: ______________
Prescribing doctor: ______________________________
Pharmacy: ______________ Prescription #: ______________
Date started: __________ Date discontinued (if any): ______________

Name: ______________________ Dosage: ______________
Number of times per day: _____ ☐ AM ☐ PM ☐ Other: ______________
Prescribing doctor: ______________________________
Pharmacy: ______________ Prescription #: ______________
Date started: __________ Date discontinued (if any): ______________

Name: ______________________________ Dosage: ________________
Number of times per day: _____ ☐ AM ☐ PM ☐ Other: ________________
Prescribing doctor: ______________________________________
Pharmacy: ________________ Prescription #: ________________
Date started: ____________ Date discontinued (if any): ________________

Name: ______________________________ Dosage: ________________
Number of times per day: _____ ☐ AM ☐ PM ☐ Other: ________________
Prescribing doctor: ______________________________________
Pharmacy: ________________ Prescription #: ________________
Date started: ____________ Date discontinued (if any): ________________

Over-the-Counter (OTC) Medications

Name: ______________________________ Dosage: ________________
Number of times per day: _____ ☐ AM ☐ PM ☐ Other: ________________
Date started: ____________ Date discontinued (if any): ________________

Name: ______________________________ Dosage: ________________
Number of times per day: _____ ☐ AM ☐ PM ☐ Other: ________________
Date started: ____________ Date discontinued (if any): ________________

Name: ______________________________ Dosage: ________________
Number of times per day: _____ ☐ AM ☐ PM ☐ Other: ________________
Date started: ____________ Date discontinued (if any): ________________

Vitamins and Supplements

Name: ______________________________ Dosage: ________________
Number of times per day: _____ ☐ AM ☐ PM ☐ Other: ________________
Date started: ____________ Date discontinued (if any): ________________

Name: ______________________________ Dosage: ________________
Number of times per day: _____ ☐ AM ☐ PM ☐ Other: ________________
Date started: ____________ Date discontinued (if any): ________________

Name: ______________________________ Dosage: ________________
Number of times per day: _____ ☐ AM ☐ PM ☐ Other: ________________
Date started: ____________ Date discontinued (if any): ________________

MY FINANCIAL ACCOUNTS

Use this section to enable your loved ones to locate all of your assets quickly and easily. This will make the settlement of your estate a much smoother process. It will also help ensure that your instructions are properly carried out.

Financial institution name: ______________________________

Account number: ______________________________

Account type: ☐ Checking ☐ Savings ☐ CD ☐ Brokerage ☐ Mutual fund
☐ Money market ☐ Safe deposit ☐ Other: ______________

Phone: ______________ Website: ______________________

Login username: ______________ Password: ______________

Name(s) on the account: ______________________________

Are any automatic deposits or withdrawals made to or from this account? ☐ Yes ☐ No

Financial institution name: ______________________________

Account number: ______________________________

Account type: ☐ Checking ☐ Savings ☐ CD ☐ Brokerage ☐ Mutual fund
☐ Money market ☐ Safe deposit ☐ Other: ______________

Phone: ______________ Website: ______________________

Login username: ______________ Password: ______________

Name(s) on the account: ______________________________

Are any automatic deposits or withdrawals made to or from this account? ☐ Yes ☐ No

Financial institution name: ______________________________

Account number: ______________________________

Account type: ☐ Checking ☐ Savings ☐ CD ☐ Brokerage ☐ Mutual fund
☐ Money market ☐ Safe deposit ☐ Other: ______________

Phone: ______________ Website: ______________________

Login username: ______________ Password: ______________

Name(s) on the account: ______________________________

Are any automatic deposits or withdrawals made to or from this account? ☐ Yes ☐ No

Financial institution name: ______________________________

Account number: ______________________________

Account type: ☐ Checking ☐ Savings ☐ CD ☐ Brokerage ☐ Mutual fund
☐ Money market ☐ Safe deposit ☐ Other: ______________

Phone: ______________ Website: ______________________

Login username: ______________ Password: ______________

Name(s) on the account: ______________________________

Are any automatic deposits or withdrawals made to or from this account? ☐ Yes ☐ No

Retirement Accounts

Company name: ____________________

Phone: ____________ Account #: ____________

Plan type: ☐ IRA ☐ Roth IRA ☐ 401(k) ☐ 403(b) ☐ Pension

☐ Profit sharing ☐ SEP ☐ Other: ____________

Owner of the plan: ____________________

Beneficiary of the plan: ____________________

Are you currently taking any distributions from this plan? ☐ Yes ☐ No

Company name: ____________________

Phone: ____________ Account #: ____________

Plan type: ☐ IRA ☐ Roth IRA ☐ 401(k) ☐ 403(b) ☐ Pension

☐ Profit sharing ☐ SEP ☐ Other: ____________

Owner of the plan: ____________________

Beneficiary of the plan: ____________________

Are you currently taking any distributions from this plan? ☐ Yes ☐ No

Company name: ____________________

Phone: ____________ Account #: ____________

Plan type: ☐ IRA ☐ Roth IRA ☐ 401(k) ☐ 403(b) ☐ Pension

☐ Profit sharing ☐ SEP ☐ Other: ____________

Owner of the plan: ____________________

Beneficiary of the plan: ____________________

Are you currently taking any distributions from this plan? ☐ Yes ☐ No

Company name: ____________________

Phone: ____________ Account #: ____________

Plan type: ☐ IRA ☐ Roth IRA ☐ 401(k) ☐ 403(b) ☐ Pension

☐ Profit sharing ☐ SEP ☐ Other: ____________

Owner of the plan: ____________________

Beneficiary of the plan: ____________________

Are you currently taking any distributions from this plan? ☐ Yes ☐ No

Company name: ____________________

Phone: ____________ Account #: ____________

Plan type: ☐ IRA ☐ Roth IRA ☐ 401(k) ☐ 403(b) ☐ Pension

☐ Profit sharing ☐ SEP ☐ Other: ____________

Owner of the plan: ____________________

Beneficiary of the plan: ____________________

Are you currently taking any distributions from this plan? ☐ Yes ☐ No

MONEY I OWE

Lender name: ______________________________
Loan type: ☐ Mortgage ☐ Auto ☐ Student ☐ Other: ______________
Account number: ______________________________
Annual percentage rate: __________ Payoff date: ______________
Phone: __________ Website: ______________
Login username: __________ Password: ______________
Location of documents: ______________________________

Lender name: ______________________________
Loan type: ☐ Mortgage ☐ Auto ☐ Student ☐ Other: ______________
Account number: ______________________________
Annual percentage rate: __________ Payoff date: ______________
Phone: __________ Website: ______________
Login username: __________ Password: ______________
Location of documents: ______________________________

Lender name: ______________________________
Loan type: ☐ Mortgage ☐ Auto ☐ Student ☐ Other: ______________
Account number: ______________________________
Annual percentage rate: __________ Payoff date: ______________
Phone: __________ Website: ______________
Login username: __________ Password: ______________
Location of documents: ______________________________

Lender name: ______________________________
Loan type: ☐ Mortgage ☐ Auto ☐ Student ☐ Other: ______________
Account number: ______________________________
Annual percentage rate: __________ Payoff date: ______________
Phone: __________ Website: ______________
Login username: __________ Password: ______________
Location of documents: ______________________________

Lender name: ______________________________
Loan type: ☐ Mortgage ☐ Auto ☐ Student ☐ Other: ______________
Account number: ______________________________
Annual percentage rate: __________ Payoff date: ______________
Phone: __________ Website: ______________
Login username: __________ Password: ______________
Location of documents: ______________________________

My Credit and Debit Cards

Company name: ______________________________

Account number: ____________________ PIN number: ____________

Phone: ____________ Website: ____________________

Login username: ____________ Password: ____________

Company name: ______________________________

Account number: ____________________ PIN number: ____________

Phone: ____________ Website: ____________________

Login username: ____________ Password: ____________

Company name: ______________________________

Account number: ____________________ PIN number: ____________

Phone: ____________ Website: ____________________

Login username: ____________ Password: ____________

MONEY OWED TO ME

Name of person/entity who owes money: ____________________

Original amount: ____________ Outstanding balance: ____________

Due date: ________ Is there a promissory note or written agreement? ☐ Yes ☐ No

Location of documents: ____________________

Name of person/entity who owes money: ____________________

Original amount: ____________ Outstanding balance: ____________

Due date: ________ Is there a promissory note or written agreement? ☐ Yes ☐ No

Location of documents: ____________________

Name of person/entity who owes money: ____________________

Original amount: ____________ Outstanding balance: ____________

Due date: ________ Is there a promissory note or written agreement? ☐ Yes ☐ No

Location of documents: ____________________

Name of person/entity who owes money: ____________________

Original amount: ____________ Outstanding balance: ____________

Due date: ________ Is there a promissory note or written agreement? ☐ Yes ☐ No

Location of documents: ____________________

MY INSURANCE

Life Insurance

Insurance company name: ____________________

Policy #: ____________________ Phone: ____________________

Type: ☐ Term ☐ Whole life ☐ Variable ☐ Universal ☐ Other: ____________________

Owner: ____________________ Person insured: ____________________

Death benefit amount: ____________________ Cash value? ☐ Yes ☐ No

Primary beneficiary: ____________________

Secondary beneficiary: ____________________

Location of documents: ____________________

Insurance company name: ____________________

Policy #: ____________________ Phone: ____________________

Type: ☐ Term ☐ Whole life ☐ Variable ☐ Universal ☐ Other: ____________________

Owner: ____________________ Person insured: ____________________

Death benefit amount: ____________________ Cash value? ☐ Yes ☐ No

Primary beneficiary: ____________________

Secondary beneficiary: ____________________

Location of documents: ____________________

Long-Term Care Insurance

Insurance company name: ____________________

Policy #: ____________________ Policy holder: ____________________

Phone: ____________________ Website: ____________________

Login username: ____________________ Password: ____________________

Location of documents: ____________________

Insurance company name: ____________________

Policy #: ____________________ Policy holder: ____________________

Phone: ____________________ Website: ____________________

Login username: ____________________ Password: ____________________

Location of documents: ____________________

Vehicle Insurance

Insurance company name: ______________________________
Vehicle make/model/year: ______________________________
Policy #: ______________ Policy holder: ______________
Billing cycle: __________ Premium: __________ Deductible: __________
Phone: ______________ Website: ______________
Login username: ______________ Password: ______________
Location of documents: ______________________________

Insurance company name: ______________________________
Vehicle make/model/year: ______________________________
Policy #: ______________ Policy holder: ______________
Billing cycle: __________ Premium: __________ Deductible: __________
Phone: ______________ Website: ______________
Login username: ______________ Password: ______________
Location of documents: ______________________________

Homeowner's/Renter's Insurance

Insurance company name: ______________________________
Policy #: ______________ Escrowed? ☐ Yes ☐ No
Billing cycle: __________ Premium: __________ Deductible: __________
Phone: ______________ Website: ______________
Login username: ______________ Password: ______________
Location of documents: ______________________________

Insurance company name: ______________________________
Policy #: ______________ Escrowed? ☐ Yes ☐ No
Billing cycle: __________ Premium: __________ Deductible: __________
Phone: ______________ Website: ______________
Login username: ______________ Password: ______________
Location of documents: ______________________________

Flood Insurance

Insurance company name: ______________________________
Policy #: ______________________________
Billing cycle: __________ Premium: __________ Deductible: __________
Phone: ______________ Website: ______________
Login username: ______________ Password: ______________
Location of documents: ______________________________

MY ANNUITIES

Company name: ______________________________

Account number: ______________________________

Phone: ____________________ Website: ____________________

Owner: ____________________ Annuitant: ____________________

Face amount: ____________________ Beneficiary: ____________________

Are you receiving distributions from this annuity contract? ☐ Yes ☐ No

Company name: ______________________________

Account number: ______________________________

Phone: ____________________ Website: ____________________

Owner: ____________________ Annuitant: ____________________

Face amount: ____________________ Beneficiary: ____________________

Are you receiving distributions from this annuity contract? ☐ Yes ☐ No

MY BUSINESS INTERESTS

Name of business: ______________________________

Type of entity: ☐ Sole proprietor ☐ Corporation ☐ Partnership ☐ LLC

Owners, partners, or members: ______________________________

Your percentage of ownership: _____%

Are there shareholder, partnership, buy-sell, or other agreements in place? ☐ Yes ☐ No

Name of business: ______________________________

Type of entity: ☐ Sole proprietor ☐ Corporation ☐ Partnership ☐ LLC

Owners, partners, or members: ______________________________

Your percentage of ownership: _____%

Are there shareholder, partnership, buy-sell, or other agreements in place? ☐ Yes ☐ No

Name of business: ______________________________

Type of entity: ☐ Sole proprietor ☐ Corporation ☐ Partnership ☐ LLC

Owners, partners, or members: ______________________________

Your percentage of ownership: _____%

Are there shareholder, partnership, buy-sell, or other agreements in place? ☐ Yes ☐ No

MY REAL ESTATE

Primary Residence

Address: ______________________________

County: ______________ Property/Parcel ID: ______________

Owner(s): ______________________________

Are there mortgages on this property? ☐ Yes ☐ No

If "yes," name and address of lender: ______________________________

____

Location of documents: ______________________________

Other Real Estate

Address of property: ______________________________

County: ______________ Property/Parcel ID: ______________

Owner(s): ______________________________

Type of property: ☐ Residential ☐ Commercial ☐ Farm ☐ Vacant land ☐ Time-share

Are there mortgages on this property? ☐ Yes ☐ No

If "yes," name and address of lender: ______________________________

____

Location of documents: ______________________________

Address of property: ______________________________

County: ______________ Property/Parcel ID: ______________

Owner(s): ______________________________

Type of property: ☐ Residential ☐ Commercial ☐ Farm ☐ Vacant land ☐ Time-share

Are there mortgages on this property? ☐ Yes ☐ No

If "yes," name and address of lender: ______________________________

____

Location of documents: ______________________________

Address of property: ______________________________

County: ______________ Property/Parcel ID: ______________

Owner(s): ______________________________

Type of property: ☐ Residential ☐ Commercial ☐ Farm ☐ Vacant land ☐ Time-share

Are there mortgages on this property? ☐ Yes ☐ No

If "yes," name and address of lender: ______________________________

____

Location of documents: ______________________________

MY VEHICLES

Make: ______________________ Model: ______________________ Year: ____________________

License plate number: __________________ VIN: ____________________________________

Title holder: ____

Location of title: ____

Make: ______________________ Model: ______________________ Year: ____________________

License plate number: __________________ VIN: ____________________________________

Title holder: ____

Location of title: ____

Make: ______________________ Model: ______________________ Year: ____________________

License plate number: __________________ VIN: ____________________________________

Title holder: ____

Location of title: ____

MY PERSONAL PROPERTY

Item: ____

Description: ____

Location: _______________________________ Value: _________________________________

Item: ____

Description: ____

Location: _______________________________ Value: _________________________________

Item: ____

Description: ____

Location: _______________________________ Value: _________________________________

Item: ____

Description: ____

Location: _______________________________ Value: _________________________________

Item: ______________________________

Description: ______________________________

Location: ______________________ Value: ______________________

Item: ______________________________

Description: ______________________________

Location: ______________________ Value: ______________________

Item: ______________________________

Description: ______________________________

Location: ______________________ Value: ______________________

Item: ______________________________

Description: ______________________________

Location: ______________________ Value: ______________________

Item: ______________________________

Description: ______________________________

Location: ______________________ Value: ______________________

Item: ______________________________

Description: ______________________________

Location: ______________________ Value: ______________________

Item: ______________________________

Description: ______________________________

Location: ______________________ Value: ______________________

Item: ______________________________

Description: ______________________________

Location: ______________________ Value: ______________________

Item: ______________________________

Description: ______________________________

Location: ______________________ Value: ______________________

MY ONLINE ACCOUNTS AND PASSWORDS

E-mail Accounts

E-mail address: ______________________________
Website address: ______________________________
Password: ______________________________

E-mail address: ______________________________
Website address: ______________________________
Password: ______________________________

Other Accounts

Website: ______________________________
Username: ______________________________
Password: ______________________________
Notes: ______________________________

Website: ______________________________
Username: ______________________________
Password: ______________________________
Notes: ______________________________

Website: ______________________________
Username: ______________________________
Password: ______________________________
Notes: ______________________________

Website: ______________________________
Username: ______________________________
Password: ______________________________
Notes: ______________________________

Website: ______________________________
Username: ______________________________
Password: ______________________________
Notes: ______________________________

Website: ______________________________

Username: ______________________________

Password: ______________________________

Notes: ______________________________

Website: ______________________________

Username: ______________________________

Password: ______________________________

Notes: ______________________________

Website: ______________________________

Username: ______________________________

Password: ______________________________

Notes: ______________________________

Website: ______________________________

Username: ______________________________

Password: ______________________________

Notes: ______________________________

Website: ______________________________

Username: ______________________________

Password: ______________________________

Notes: ______________________________

Website: ______________________________

Username: ______________________________

Password: ______________________________

Notes: ______________________________

Website: ______________________________

Username: ______________________________

Password: ______________________________

Notes: ______________________________

Website: ______________________________

Username: ______________________________

Password: ______________________________

Notes: ______________________________

MY MEMORIAL INSTRUCTIONS

Share your wishes regarding your funeral services, burial, or cremation. If you have preplanned or prepaid for these services, it is important that your loved ones know. You might also want to specify the details of your memorial service or provide guidelines on expenditures.

Disposition of My Remains

After my death, I wish to be: ☐ Buried ☐ Cremated ☐ Other: ____________________

If cremated, I wish to have the following person(s) take responsibility/possession of my remains: ____________________

I have already purchased a burial plot: ☐ Yes ☐ No

Name of cemetery: ____________________

Address: ____________________

Phone: ____________________ Location of deed: ____________________

Funeral Home

This is the funeral home that should handle my final arrangements.

Name of funeral home: ____________________

Address: ____________________

Phone: ____________________ Funeral director: ____________________

Memorial Service

For my memorial service, I prefer the following:

Location: ____________________

Who should conduct the service: ____________________

Music: ____________________

____

Readings: ____________________

Flowers: ____________________

Pallbearers: ____________________

____

Contributions designated to: ____________________

____

LETTER OF INSTRUCTIONS

Use the space below to write a personal letter of instructions to your loved ones about your desires for your funeral service and burial arrangements. Be as detailed as you like.

FAMILY AND FRIENDS TO BE CONTACTED

List those friends and relatives you would want to have notified in the event of your death.

Name: ______________________ Relationship: ______________________
Address: ______________________
Phone: ______________________ E-mail: ______________________

Name: ______________________ Relationship: ______________________
Address: ______________________
Phone: ______________________ E-mail: ______________________

Name: ______________________ Relationship: ______________________
Address: ______________________
Phone: ______________________ E-mail: ______________________

Name: ______________________ Relationship: ______________________
Address: ______________________
Phone: ______________________ E-mail: ______________________

Name: ______________________ Relationship: ______________________
Address: ______________________
Phone: ______________________ E-mail: ______________________

Name: ______________________ Relationship: ______________________
Address: ______________________
Phone: ______________________ E-mail: ______________________

Name: ______________________ Relationship: ______________________
Address: ______________________
Phone: ______________________ E-mail: ______________________

Name: ______________________ Relationship: ______________________
Address: ______________________
Phone: ______________________ E-mail: ______________________

Name: ______________________ Relationship: ______________________
Address: ______________________
Phone: ______________________ E-mail: ______________________

Name: ______________________ Relationship: ______________________
Address: ______________________
Phone: ______________________ E-mail: ______________________

Name: ______________________ Relationship: ______________________
Address: ______________________
Phone: ______________________ E-mail: ______________________

Name: ______________________ Relationship: ______________________
Address: ______________________
Phone: ______________________ E-mail: ______________________

Name: ______________________ Relationship: ______________________
Address: ______________________
Phone: ______________________ E-mail: ______________________

Name: ______________________ Relationship: ______________________
Address: ______________________
Phone: ______________________ E-mail: ______________________

Name: ______________________ Relationship: ______________________
Address: ______________________
Phone: ______________________ E-mail: ______________________

Name: ______________________ Relationship: ______________________
Address: ______________________
Phone: ______________________ E-mail: ______________________

Name: ______________________ Relationship: ______________________
Address: ______________________
Phone: ______________________ E-mail: ______________________

Name: ______________________ Relationship: ______________________
Address: ______________________
Phone: ______________________ E-mail: ______________________

Name: ______________________ Relationship: ______________________
Address: ______________________
Phone: ______________________ E-mail: ______________________

ADVISERS AND OTHER ENTITIES TO BE CONTACTED

List professional advisers and entities with whom you do business to be notified in the event of your death.

Attorney: ______________________ Firm name: ______________________
Phone: ______________________ E-mail: ______________________

Attorney: ______________________ Firm name: ______________________
Phone: ______________________ E-mail: ______________________

Accountant: ______________________ Firm name: ______________________
Phone: ______________________ E-mail: ______________________

Auto/home/liability insurance agent: ______________________
Company name: ______________________
Phone: ______________________ E-mail: ______________________

Auto/home/liability insurance agent: ______________________
Company name: ______________________
Phone: ______________________ E-mail: ______________________

Financial adviser: ______________________ Firm name: ______________________
Phone: ______________________ E-mail: ______________________

Financial adviser: ______________________ Firm name: ______________________
Phone: ______________________ E-mail: ______________________

Bank or credit union: ______________________
Phone: ______________________ E-mail: ______________________

Bank or credit union: ______________________
Phone: ______________________ E-mail: ______________________

Financial institution: ______________________
Phone: ______________________ E-mail: ______________________

Financial institution: ______________________
Phone: ______________________ E-mail: ______________________

Doctor: ______________________
Phone: ______________________ E-mail: ______________________

Doctor: ______________________________

Phone: ______________ E-mail: ______________

Doctor: ______________________________

Phone: ______________ E-mail: ______________

Doctor: ______________________________

Phone: ______________ E-mail: ______________

Doctor: ______________________________

Phone: ______________ E-mail: ______________

Dentist: ______________________________

Phone: ______________ E-mail: ______________

Charitable concerns: ______________________________

Phone: ______________ E-mail: ______________

Charitable concerns: ______________________________

Phone: ______________ E-mail: ______________

Pastor/priest/rabbi: ______________________________

Church/synagogue: ______________________________

Phone: ______________ E-mail: ______________

Pastor/priest/rabbi: ______________________________

Church/synagogue: ______________________________

Phone: ______________ E-mail: ______________

Employer or business partner: ______________________________

Phone: ______________ E-mail: ______________

Employer or business partner: ______________________________

Phone: ______________ E-mail: ______________

Life insurance agent: ______________________________

Company: ______________________________

Phone: ______________ E-mail: ______________

Trustee: ______________________ Relationship: ______________________

Phone: ______________________ E-mail: ______________________

Trustee: ______________________ Relationship: ______________________

Phone: ______________________ E-mail: ______________________

Trustee: ______________________ Relationship: ______________________

Phone: ______________________ E-mail: ______________________

Trustee: ______________________ Relationship: ______________________

Phone: ______________________ E-mail: ______________________

Pension/retirement fund contact: ______________________

Phone: ______________________ E-mail: ______________________

Government Entities

Health & Human Services (Medicare/Medicaid)

Phone: ______________________ E-mail: ______________________

Internal Revenue Service

Phone: ______________________ E-mail: ______________________

Post office

Address: ______________________

Phone: ______________________ E-mail: ______________________

Social Security Administration

Phone: ______________________ E-mail: ______________________

LOCATION OF IMPORTANT DOCUMENTS

The following list and chart will help you and/or your loved ones find all of your important documents. Documents that would be difficult, expensive, or impossible to replace should be stored in a safe-deposit box or waterproof/fireproof home safe. Some of your important papers might be stored with your professional advisers. Fill in the spaces below to list the location of your safe-deposit boxes, home storage locations, and advisers. On the chart that lists these locations on page 32, write the appropriate number in the boxes indicating where the item is stored.

Safe-Deposit Boxes

Safety-deposit box #1

Bank name: ____________________

Address: ____________________

Box number: __________ Location of key: __________

Safety-deposit box #2

Bank name: ____________________

Address: ____________________

Box number: __________ Location of key: __________

Home Storage Locations

Location #1: ____________________

Location #2: ____________________

Location #3: ____________________

Location #4: ____________________

Attorney: ____________________

Accountant: ____________________

Financial adviser: ____________________

Others: ____________________

____

____

____

DOCUMENTS LOCATION CHART

Write the corresponding number in the box indicating where the item is stored.

1. Safe-deposit box #1
2. Safe-deposit box #2
3. Home #1
4. Home #2
5. Home #3
6. Home #4
7. Attorney
8. Accountant
9. Financial adviser
10. Other: ____________

____

____

- ☐ 401(k) documents
- ☐ Adoption papers
- ☐ Annuities
- ☐ Bank stmts.
- ☐ Bills of sale
- ☐ Birth certificate
- ☐ Bonds
- ☐ Cemetery plot deed
- ☐ Certificates of deposit
- ☐ Checkbook(s)
- ☐ Citizenship papers
- ☐ Contracts
- ☐ Corp./partnership papers
- ☐ Credit card info
- ☐ Divorce papers
- ☐ Estate planning docs
- ☐ Flood ins.
- ☐ Health ins.
- ☐ Homeowner's ins.
- ☐ Income tax returns
- ☐ Investment account stmts.
- ☐ IRA docs
- ☐ Leases
- ☐ Letters of instruction
- ☐ Life insurance
- ☐ Living will
- ☐ Loans payable to you
- ☐ Long-term care ins.
- ☐ Marriage certificate
- ☐ Military papers
- ☐ Mortgage papers
- ☐ Passport
- ☐ Pension plan
- ☐ Power of attorney (financial)
- ☐ Power of attorney (health)
- ☐ Property deed(s)
- ☐ Property tax records
- ☐ Savings book(s)
- ☐ Social Security card
- ☐ Stock certificates
- ☐ Tax records (bus.)
- ☐ Tax records (pers.)
- ☐ Title insurance
- ☐ Vehicle ins.
- ☐ Vehicle title
- ☐ W-2s, 1099s
- ☐ Will or Trust